THE OFFICIAL
ENGLAND RUGBY
ANNUAL 2014

Written by Martin Johnston

Designed by Brian Thomson

A Grange Publication

ISBN 978 1 908925 55 8

£7.99

England Rugby

CONTENTS

England
Rugby

WELCOME TO THE OFFICIAL ENGLAND RUGBY ANNUAL 2014

We've got a fantastic edition for you this year, crammed full of fascinating info and top pictures of all your favourite England players.

As ever 2013 was an eventful year for Stuart Lancaster and his England team which left plenty for us to discuss. But we didn't stop with the elite squad. There are stacks of exclusive features on all the important stuff like the England Saxons, the World Cup-Winning England Under 20s and other England sides.

There are profiles of stars like Mike Brown, Tom Youngs and Geoff Parling and you'll also catch up with some of the emerging stars in the famous white jersey, as well as getting all the goss' on what the England boys get up to off the pitch.

You can test your friends with The Big England Quiz and then test yourself with a cracking Wordsearch and the ever popular Spot the Ball. There's something for every England Rugby fan in this year's annual. So turn the page and enjoy!

RBS 6 NATIONS
2013 ROUND-UP

The 2013 RBS 6 Nations was a case of so near and yet so far for England for the second season in a row. Once more the last hurdle proved too much.

A record loss to a fired-up Welsh team saw the hard work of the previous games undone.

FINAL TABLE

	W	D	L	T	F	A	Pts
1. Wales	4	0	1	9	122	66	8
2. England	4	0	1	5	94	78	8
3. Scotland	2	0	3	7	98	107	4
4. Italy	2	0	3	5	75	111	4
5. Ireland	1	1	3	5	72	81	3
6. France	1	1	3	6	73	91	0

WEEKEND ONE

Debutant Billy Twelvetrees took the headlines with a try in England's composed 38-18 win at home to retain the Calcutta Cup. Chris Ashton, Geoff Parling and Danny Care also grabbed tries as Owen Farrell landed 18 points with the boot. Italy scored a famous home victory 23-18 over France, while Wales lost 22-30 at home to Ireland.

WEEKEND TWO

An impressive, gritty 12-6 victory in Dublin, gained courtesy of three Owen Farrell penalties, gave England justified hope for the rest of the tournament. Wales finally got back on track with an impressive 16-6 win in Paris, while Scotland saw off Italy with a 34-10 home win.

WEEKEND THREE

The third round saw another impressive display from Lancaster's men who condemned France to their third straight defeat. Manu Tuilagi scored a try with Owen Farrell landing four penalties and Toby Flood adding two more late on. Wales' rehabilitation continued with a 26-9 victory in Rome, while Ireland's woes piled up as they lost 12-8 to Scotland at Murrayfield.

WEEKEND FOUR

A much tougher than expected Italian side made England fight for every point of their 18-11 home win. Italy scored a try but Toby Flood's six penalties saw the men in white home. France finally grabbed a point by drawing 13-13 in an amazing match against Ireland in Dublin. Wales kept up their head of steam with a 28-18 win in Edinburgh.

WEEKEND FIVE

And so to the last round and another must-win against Wales, the strongest team in Europe. But it was not to be. Wales ran out 30-3 winners, a record score for them against England as a jubilant Millennium Stadium feted their RBS 6 Nations winners. Italy gained their highest ever finish as another impressive display saw them dispatch Ireland 22-15 and condemn the Irish to fifth place. France finally found a win at home by beating Scotland 23-16, though a third place finish was some consolation for the Scots.

TWICKENHAM: HOME OF ENGLAND RUGBY

Twickenham Stadium is the proud Home of England Rugby. These days it seats an impressive 82,000 spectators and is currently the largest dedicated rugby union venue in the world.

In 1907 a ten-and-a-quarter acre market garden in Twickenham was purchased by the RFU for £5,572 12s.6d. Committee member William Williams was largely responsible for acquiring the land, against much opposition, and it became known as "Billy Williams' Cabbage Patch."

The first game was played in 1909, a battle between local sides Harlequins and Richmond, and over 100 years later all of the top international sides have played, triumphed and had their hearts broken here.

These days, Twickenham offers much more than just the best rugby. It has become a destination for fans around the world to experience the excitement of matches, sample a stadium tour or visit the brand new World Rugby Museum.

Also one of the world's greatest music venues, Twickenham has hosted the biggest names in world music from the Rolling Stones to Rihanna.

THIS IS...
THE SPIRIT OF RUGBY

THE WORLD RUGBY MUSEUM

The refurbished museum was launched in October 2013. The new look World Rugby Museum should be the first stop for visitors to Twickenham, the Home of England Rugby.

The museum is split into four main zones:

PLAY RUGBY

For younger fans the first stop should be the Play Rugby zone. This section is fully interactive and there is plenty to do, see, feel and hear! You can try kicking a penalty on the famous Twickenham pitch and find out 'What Kind of Rugby Player Are You?'

THE SPIRIT OF RUGBY

Why do so many people love rugby? Find out in the Spirit of Rugby zone by experiencing the game from grass roots right up to elite level.

RUGBY'S STORY

This zone is a fascinating journey through rugby's history. Discover how a schoolboy game became one of international sport's major spectacles.

RUGBY MOMENTS

Some of the greatest players, matches and tries of all time brought to life with a bit of the infamous humour of the game thrown in to keep you laughing.

ENGLAND'S HISTORY
ALL THE STATISTICS

Here's a round-up of all our key matches and statistics in the history of England Rugby.*

FIRST MATCH
Scotland 1 England 0 – Edinburgh 1871.

BIGGEST WIN
England 134 Romania 0 – Twickenham 2001.

BIGGEST DEFEAT
Australia 76 England 0 – Brisbane 1998.

WORLD CUP APPEARANCES
Seven.

MOST CAPS
Jason Leonard 114 (pictured here after receiving his 100th Cap!).

*As at August 2013

MOST POINTS
Jonny Wilkinson 1,246.

MOST TRIES
Rory Underwood 49.

BEST WORLD CUP RESULT
World Champions, 2003. Defeated Australia in Sydney.

England Rugby

DANNY CARE

Spot the Difference

Take a good look at these two pictures of England team members. They might look very similar at first glance. But look closely and you'll see that the bottom one has six changes.

Can you spot them all?

Answers on page 61

England
Rugby

CHRIS
ROBSHAW

The BIG England Rugby Quiz

1. In which city was the 2011 Rugby World Cup final held?
2. And who were the finalists?
3. Which two countries compete for The Bledisloe Cup?
4. Which of England's international opponents play in sky blue and white shirts?
5. At which stadium will the 2015 Rugby World Cup final be held?
6. What is a 'grubber'?
7. How does an assistant referee indicate a penalty goal or conversion has been scored?
8. Which England player scored a try on his debut against Scotland in the 2013 RBS 6 Nations match?
9. Which of England's international opponents has a junior team known as 'The Baby Boks'?
10. Which English club side plays at the famous Welford Road ground?
11. Which of England's international opponents play in gold shirts?
12. Which of England's international opponents' badge features a cockerel?
13. What is the current seating capacity of Twickenham Stadium?
14. What number does a hooker traditionally wear?
15. Which of England's international opponents' badge features a silver fern?
16. Who was England's top points scorer in the 2013 RBS 6 Nations?
17. What is the minimum number of players required to form a lineout?
18. England's Mike Brown plays for which club?
19. England and which other country compete for the Calcutta Cup?
20. What number does an outside centre traditionally wear?

Answers on page 61

England Rugby

ENGLAND **BELIEVE** ENGLAND **BELONG** ENGLAND **BE THERE**

love RUGBY?

Does someone you love love rugby?

There's no better gift than membership of The England Rugby Supporter Club or the Junior Supporters Club.

Members get a range of benefits including access to tickets, exclusive competitions and offers plus much more. Junior members also have the chance to run out with the England team as a mascot.

For more details on both clubs go to RFU.com/fanzone or call 0871 663 1863.

JOIN TODAY

ADULTS £39 / JUNIORS £5

VISIT RFU.COM/FANZONE
CALL 0871 663 1863

INVEST IN RUGBY

The England rose is an official registered trade mark of the Rugby Football Union.

FROM TINY ACORNS

'Mighty oaks grow from tiny acorns', goes the saying.

So where did some of the mighty oaks of the England elite squad begin their careers?

Name: Billy Twelvetrees
Position: Centre
Began at: Haywards Heath RFC (currently in London 1 South)

Name: Freddie Burns
Position: Fly half
Began at: Avon RFC (currently in Tribute Western Counties North)

Name: Calum Clark
Position: Flanker
Began at: Darlington RFC (currently in North 1 East)

Name: Owen Farrell
Position: Fly Half
Began at: Wigan St. Patricks (Rugby League). His first Rugby Union club was Saracens.

Name: Alex Corbisiero
Position: Prop
Began at: KCS Old Boys (currently in London 2 South West)

IN FOCUS: MAKO VUNIPOLA

A meteoric rise from the start of the 2012-13 season saw Mako Vunipola's form for Saracens lead to a full England call up and a place on the 2013 British & Irish Lions tour of Australia.

The young prop is part of a famous Tongan rugby dynasty and made his England debut at Twickenham against Fiji after only 15 Aviva Premiership appearances. He came off the bench seven times in all before making his first start against Italy in March 2013.

His unstoppable rise to the very top flight of international rugby continued with two appearances from the bench for the Lions, before making his debut for them in the second test in Brisbane.

Mako's father Fe'ao was a 32-cap international for Tonga who emigrated to Wales in 1998 to play for Pontypool. His grandfather and six of his uncles have also represented Tonga.

Mako moved to Saracens after spells at Bristol and Bedford Blues. He first played rugby at Griffithstown Junior School in Pontypool before continuing his education at West Monmouth School and those two famous nurseries of the game, Castle School and Millfield.

Two years each in the England U18 and U20 squads brought him his first international success, including tours of Argentina and South Africa and a 6 Nations Grand Slam which saw him force his way over for tries against Ireland and Scotland.

Did You Know?

Mako's brother, Viliami aka 'Billy', played with him at England U18 level and also seems destined for elite success.

FOUR
TO WATCH

CALUM CLARK

Born in Stockton-on-Tees flanker Calum Clark first played for Darlington RFC before moving south to Yorkshire to join the Leeds Carnegie Academy at the age of 14. He has been clocking up major achievements ever since and none of his former coaches, who include Brian Ashton, will have been surprised to see him in an England elite squad.

The Northampton Saints flanker is sure to figure in Stuart Lancaster's future plans.

GEORGE ROBSON

A key figure in the England Saxons squad for 2012-13, the Harlequins lock is another future contender for a Six Nations spot.

Hailing from Stourbridge, apart from an invaluable but short spell in South Africa with Natal, he has played all his senior rugby at Quins where he is now a first choice at lock.

Conor O'Shea, Director of Rugby at the club, says of Robson, "He is one of the most competitive people I have come across."

JOEL TOMKINS

Older brother of Rugby League's hottest property, Sam Tomkins, Joel also started in the 13-man code. He played with his brother at Wigan Warriors and went on to make 125 appearances for them before switching to Saracens.

He has shown his versatility by playing across the back line for the London club and is also viewed as a utility back by England's elite management team.

With a couple of Saxons caps under his belt, he was one of the first names on the squad list of the 2013 tour of Argentina but an unfortunate ankle injury ruled him out.

ELLIOT DALY

Elliot Daly of London Wasps has ten England U20 caps under his belt and came to prominence with solid performances for the Barbarians twice in June 2013.

He is a product of Whitgift School and the London Wasps Academy. He was also a key player for both the England U16 and U18 teams and scored for the latter in a 33-16 win over France at Newbury in 2010.

Also an accomplished cricketer, he rates fellow centre Brian O'Driscoll as the player he most admires.

IN FOCUS: TOM YOUNGS

Leicester Tigers hooker Tom Youngs made his test debut against Fiji in the QBE international in November 2012. He then went on to start seven of England's next eight games.

He joined his brother Ben in the game against Fiji as they became the first siblings since the Armitages in 2009 to play for England. The brothers then went on to play for the British & Irish Lions together on the successful tour of Australia in summer 2013.

Born in Norwich and educated at Gresham's in nearby Holt, Tom was originally a robust, tough-tackling centre. However, while on loan at Nottingham former Leicester head coach Heyneke Meyer suggested he should try being a hooker and he has never looked back since.

He joined Ben at Leicester in 2006 and played a handful of Premiership games scoring a try against Leeds in 2007. His loan period at Nottingham started in 2009 and switching to the No.2 jersey he ended up playing 60 games and winning the accolade of Players' Player of the Year.

He has represented England at U16, U18 and U20 and played in the IRB Sevens World Series in 2007.

Did You Know?

Tom and Ben learnt their rugby from father Nick, an England scrum half capped six times in the eighties.

IN FOCUS: MIKE BROWN

Mike Brown proved such an explosive force for England Saxons that his climb to the top level of the Elite Squad became inevitable. The Harlequins full back is used by Stuart Lancaster in both the No.15 shirt and on the wing such is his fitness and versatility.

Born in Southampton he was educated at Peter Symonds College in Winchester and Wyvern College in Salisbury. His first representative appearance was for Dorset & Wiltshire U14s and he progressed to South West U18s before joining the Harlequins Academy in 2002.

Brown made his Quins senior debut against Doncaster Knights in 2005 and ended up running in seven tries in 13 National One games that season. He was the club's Young Player of the Year that year and Player of the Year the very next season.

He was a key figure in Harlequins' first ever Aviva Premiership title win in 2012 and also scored five Heineken Cup tries. By the end of the 2012-13 season he had scored 67 tries in 207 appearances.

Did You Know?
Mike was ever present for Quins in the 2007-08 season playing more minutes than any other player.

ENGLAND UNDER 20s
WORLD CHAMPIONS!

At the fourth time of asking, England U20s finally become World Champions for the first time in 2013. Having lost three previous finals - all to a seemingly invincible New Zealand - England made no mistake against Wales.

The sixth IRB Junior World Cup was staged in France and saw England drawn in a relatively tough group, which included holders South Africa and their French hosts. The group also included JWC newcomers, the USA.

England coach Nick Walshe, in his debut season with the team, saw his team get off to a flying start by beating hosts France 30-6 in the Stade Henri Desgrange.

They were brought down to earth in the next game however, as the 'Baby Boks' handed them a 31-24 defeat in the same stadium. But they bounced back in spectacular style, shutting out the USA and winning 109-0.

The defeat to South Africa meant that England qualified for the semi-finals only as best-placed runner-up and that meant a showdown with the 'Baby Blacks' of New Zealand, against whom they had never won at the JWC.

But June 18 in Vannes was to be England's day as they played out of their skins to score an impressive 33-21 win. Earlier the same day Wales U20s had delivered their own special result by narrowly edging out holders South Africa by 18-17.

So the stage was set for the first ever all European final at the JWC and the 200th ever match of the competition.

England delivered the win in a thrilling match in Vannes, despite going two tries behind and trailing 3-15 at half-time. The second half was a different matter as tries from Jack Nowell and Sam Hill and the superb kicking of Henry Slade saw them run out 23-15 victors.

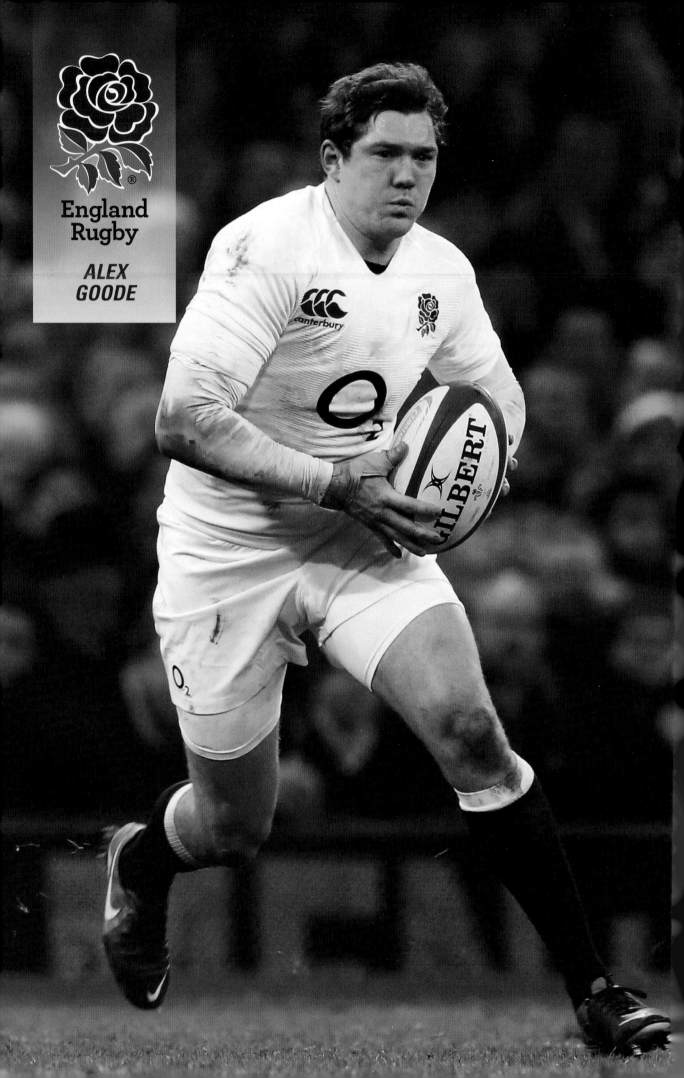

England
Rugby

*ALEX
GOODE*

Spot the Ball

Can you help Ruckley spot which is the real rugby ball in the picture below?

Answer on page 61

Meet Ruckley!

Say hello to Ruckley, the newest, keenest and most talented member of the England squad!

He's England's biggest fan, the team's best friend and a bit of a secret star.

He used to be a normal English bulldog, happy-go-lucky but a bit naughty like all bulldogs. One day he was digging under the pitch at Twickenham and he found a strange clear crystal ball with a rose inside it. This transformed him into a super dog, a super fan and England's biggest supporter!

Now he's **BIG!** He's **STRONG!** And he's **FAST!**

And Ruckley loves nothing better than playing rugby with his friends.

Watch the story behind Ruckley at **RFU.COM/Ruckley**

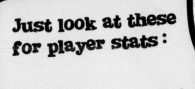

Just look at these for player stats:

Bravery .... 100%.
Courage .... 100%.
Friendliness ... 100%.
Skills .... 100%.

ENGLAND
RUGBY

IN FOCUS: GEOFF PARLING

Lock Geoff Parling, who is also an accomplished flanker at club level, had been destined to play for England ever since his first appearance at national level for the U16s. He has now played for England at every age level possible: U16, U18, U19 and U21.

In 2009-10, his debut season for Leicester Tigers, he played 30 matches and was part of the team that beat Saracens 33-26 to win the Premiership title at Twickenham.

He followed that triumph with 17 consecutive England caps, including a jubilant first try in the 2013 home win against Scotland in the 2013 Calcutta Cup match.

He moved to Leicester from Newcastle Falcons, where he had been Player of the Year and captain of their development side, playing as both lock and blind-side flanker. In all he put in 116 appearances for the Falcons before signing for the Tigers in 2009.

He received the ultimate recognition with a place on the 2013 British & Irish Lions tour to Australia and played in the two test victories.

Did You Know?

Geoff captained the 2013 Lions midweek team in their 35-0 win over the Melbourne Rebels.

England Rugby

TOBY FLOOD

Word Search

Help Ruckley find all 20 rugby-related words in the grid below.

Words can read across, upwards, downwards, backwards or even diagonally!

T	L	K	G	X	K	Y	E	L	K	C	U	R	E
H	B	L	C	L	D	R	Z	T	K	C	D	G	W
Y	C	N	M	I	K	C	L	C	A	W	D	Z	J
O	D	U	L	L	K	F	S	L	A	U	X	R	N
U	B	R	O	W	N	R	C	H	J	T	E	T	R
N	H	R	W	T	Z	U	F	R	O	K	C	K	Y
G	C	E	N	B	T	Q	V	L	N	R	T	H	E
S	A	G	V	T	W	T	S	A	G	P	T	N	L
F	O	N	A	T	C	N	L	G	S	K	K	S	T
D	C	I	T	E	Q	F	Y	M	T	N	B	J	R
R	W	W	N	C	Y	K	Q	G	N	W	N	L	A
Z	K	T	L	D	P	A	R	L	I	N	G	N	H
H	R	A	R	D	L	A	N	C	A	S	T	E	R
E	F	L	D	T	R	I	H	S	S	L	C	J	M

WINGER	CALCUTTA	BROWN	SHIRT
FALCONS	RUCKLEY	CATCH	TOUCH
LANCASTER	KICK	YOUNGS	JUDGE
SHORTS	SAINTS	HARTLEY	COACH
FLAG	FLANKER	CENTRE	PARLING

Answers on page 61

39

BROTHERS IN ARMS

ENGLAND'S YOUNG LIONS IN AUSTRALIA

England's top players all played their parts in the magnificent series win in Australia for the British & Irish Lions in 2013. None more so than the Youngs brothers, Ben and Tom, sons of England scrum half Nick.

The brothers, who both play for Leicester Tigers, became the first siblings to start a Lions test since the Scots pair of Scott and Gavin Hastings a quarter of a century ago.

They both shared in the triumph of the first test win in Brisbane as Tom started as hooker and Ben came off the bench in the 62nd minute to replace Mike Phillips.

The second test was not to be so joyous as the Lions went down by just a point in a 16-15 loss in Melbourne.

However the boys recovered from the disappointment to experience one of the great moments of British & Irish rugby as the Lions crushed the Wallabies 41-16, with their countryman Alex Corbisiero scoring a try in the first minute.

Ben was in the stands cheering Tom on, a 47th minute replacement for Richard Hibbard. But both knew they had played a big part in one of the great tours down under.

England
Rugby

CHRIS ASHTON

Guess? Who

Can you guess who the players are in the pictures below?

1

2

3

4

Answers on page 61

ENGLAND MATCH STATISTICS 2013

Here are the test match stats for England in 2013.

Included are games from the 2013 RBS 6 Nations and the tour of Argentina.

RBS 6 NATIONS 2013

England 38, Scotland 18

Twickenham, Feb 2, 2013

England Tries: Ashton, Care, Parling, Twelvetrees; **Cons:** Farrell 3; **Pens:** Farrell 4.

Scotland Tries: Hogg, Maitland; **Con:** Laidlaw; **Pens:** Laidlaw 2.

Ireland 6, England 12

Aviva Stadium, Feb 10, 2013

England Pens: Farrell 4.

Ireland Pens: O'Gara 2.

England 23, France 13

Twickenham, Feb 23, 2013

England Try: Tuilagi; **Pens:** Farrell 4, Flood 2.

France Try: Fofana; **Con:** Parra; **Pens:** Parra, Michalak.

England 18, Italy 11

Twickenham, March 10, 2013

England Pens: Flood 6.

Italy Try: McLean; **Pens:** Orquera 2.

Wales 30, England 3

Millennium Stadium, March 16, 2013

England Pen: Farrell.

Wales Tries: Cuthbert 2 **Con:** Biggar; **Pens:** Halfpenny 4, Biggar; **DG:** Biggar.

ARGENTINE TEST SERIES 2013

FIRST TEST

Argentina 3, England 32

Salta, June 8, 2013

England Tries: Strettle, Twelvetrees, Morgan, Vunipola; **Cons:** Burns 3; **Pens:** Burns 2.

Argentina Pen: Moyano.

SECOND TEST

Argentina 26, England 51

Buenos Aires, June 15, 2013

England Tries: Yarde 2, Penalty 2, Burns, Webber, Eastmond; **Cons:** Burns 4, Myler; **Pens:** Burns 2.

Argentina Tries: Montero, Leonardi; **Cons:** Moyana 2; **Pens:** Moyana 4.

England Rugby

IN FOCUS: DYLAN HARTLEY

Dylan Hartley was born in the famous rugby town of Rotorua, scene of many famous victories for the Maori and other New Zealand representative sides over various touring teams.

He learnt his rugby at Rotorua Boys High School and played a handful of games for Bay of Plenty U18s before moving to England as a teenager. In those days he was a prop but became a hooker at Northampton Saints, his current club.

While staying with relatives in Crowborough, East Sussex in 2003, Dylan was called up by an enterprising England U18s management team, having qualified by English ancestry. He returned home to New Zealand shortly after but jumped at the chance to come back and play for England U19s.

After an impressive series of games for the U19s, he was quickly drafted into the England U21 squad and made his full debut in 2007 after shining for England Saxons.

Did You Know?

Dylan has also worked with specialist coach Steve Peters who helped British cyclists Bradley Wiggins and Victoria Pendleton win gold medals at the 2012 Olympics.

ENGLAND'S SUMMER 2013 TOUR TO ARGENTINA

After the last-game heartbreak again in the RBS 6 Nations, England restored pride on their tour to Argentina in June 2013.

With first-choice players on duty in Australia with the British & Irish Lions and up against the traditionally fierce forwards of the Argentines it would be a tough ask. But Lancaster's men came through with flying colours, winning all three games on the tour.

England began by playing in Montevideo, the capital of Uruguay. Although not officially a test match, England were glad to grab a 41-21 win against a mixed team of Argentine, Uruguayan, Chilean and Brazilian players. Young Number 8, Billy Vunipola, was the pick of the England players, taking home the match ball with a hat-trick of tries.

Six days later England lined up for the much tougher proposition of the Argentina team in Salta. Again, however, they were too strong for their South American opponents, restricting them to just one penalty and claiming a 32-3 victory. Vunipola grabbed himself another try as did David Strettle, Billy Twelvetrees and Ben Morgan, while Freddie Burns showed his kicking prowess landing 10 points.

The second test in Buenos Aires saw England pile more points on Argentina in a very open game. This time England shipped 26 points but on the plus side they scored six of their own tries and Freddie Burns scored 14 more points with the boot. A 51-26 win to take home for a very satisfied squad of experienced and brand new players.

ENGLAND

AT THE RUGBY WORLD CUP SEVENS IN 2013

Just like Stuart Lancaster's men in the RBS 6 Nations, it was a case of so near and yet so far for the England Sevens team.

The RWC Sevens was held in Moscow and was the sixth time the event had been held. Wales were the defending champions having won the 2009 title in Dubai.

Head coach Ben Ryan took his charges to Moscow. Within their ranks was HSBC World Sevens Series top points and try-scorer, Dan Norton of Gloucester.

England started well and just got better. They won all three of their pool games beating Argentina, Portugal and Hong Kong. They then saw off a strong Australian challenge 21-17. A tough encounter with the ever-improving Kenyans in the semis couldn't knock them out of their stride as they triumphed 12-5 to set up a final with favourites New Zealand.

Ryan's men left nothing on the field but fell well short in the end. Runner-up medals were scant consolation for a 33-0 defeat to a team right at the top of its game.

"Within their ranks was HSBC World Sevens Series top points and try-scorer, Dan Norton of Gloucester."

PLAYER PROFILES

ALEX CORBISIERO

Club: Northampton Saints   **Position:** Prop
Height: 1.86m   **Weight:** 118kg
Caps: 18   **Points:** 0

ALEX GOODE

Club: Saracens   **Position:** Full back/Fly half
Height: 1.81m   **Weight:** 85kg
Caps: 11   **Points:** 0

BEN FODEN

Club: Northampton Saints   **Position:** Full back/Wing
Height: 1.83m   **Weight:** 93kg
Caps: 32   **Points:** 35 – 7T

BEN MORGAN

Club: Gloucester Rugby   **Position:** Number 8
Height: 1.91m   **Weight:** 116kg
Caps: 12   **Points:** 5 – 1T

BEN YOUNGS

Club: Leicester Tigers

Height: 1.78m

Caps: 33

Position: Scrum half

Weight: 92kg

Points: 30 – 6T

BILLY TWELVETREES

Club: Gloucester Rugby

Height: 1.91m

Caps: 5

Position: Centre/Flyhalf

Weight: 100kg

Points: 10 – 2T

BILLY VUNIPOLA

Club: Saracens

Height: 1.88m

Caps: 2

Position: Flanker/No.8

Weight: 126kg

Points: 5 – 1T

BRAD BARRITT

Club: Saracens

Height: 1.86m

Caps: 16

Position: Centre

Weight: 95kg

Points: 5 – 1T

PLAYER PROFILES

CHRIS ASHTON

Club: Saracens

Height: 1.82m

Caps: 34

Position: Wing

Weight: 92kg

Points: 85 – 17T

CHRIS ROBSHAW

Club: Harlequins

Height: 1.88m

Caps: 17

Position: Back row

Weight: 110kg

Points: 0

CHRISTIAN WADE

Club: London Wasps

Height: 1.78m

Caps: 1

Position: Wing

Weight: 81kg

Points: 0

COURTNEY LAWES

Club: Northampton Saints

Height: 2m

Caps: 22

Position: Lock/Flanker

Weight: 111kg

Points: 0

DAN COLE

Club: Leicester Tigers   **Position:** Prop
Height: 1.89m   **Weight:** 118kg
Caps: 40   **Points:** 5 – 1T

DANNY CARE

Club: Harlequins   **Position:** Scrum half
Height: 1.74m   **Weight:** 85kg
Caps: 41   **Points:** 28 – 5T, 1 DG

DAVID ATTWOOD

Club: Bath Rugby   **Position:** Lock
Height: 2.01m   **Weight:** 118kg
Caps: 4   **Points:** 0

DAVID WILSON

Club: Bath Rugby   **Position:** Prop
Height: 1.87m   **Weight:** 112kg
Caps: 28   **Points:** 0

PLAYER PROFILES

DYLAN HARTLEY

Club: Northampton Saints   **Position:** Hooker
Height: 1.85m   **Weight:** 110kg
Caps: 47   **Points:** 5 – 1T

FREDDIE BURNS

Club: Gloucester Rugby   **Position:** Fly half
Height: 1.88m   **Weight:** 80kg
Caps: 3   **Points:** 37 – 1T, 7C, 6PG

GEOFF PARLING

Club: Leicester Tigers   **Position:** Lock/Flanker
Height: 1.98m   **Weight:** 114kg
Caps: 17   **Points:** 5 – 1T

JOE LAUNCHBURY

Club: London Wasps   **Position:** Lock/Flanker
Height: 1.98m   **Weight:** 115kg
Caps: 11   **Points:** 0

JOE MARLER

Club: Harlequins   **Position:** Prop
Height: 1.84m   **Weight:** 110kg
Caps: 12   **Points:** 0

KYLE EASTMOND

Club: Bath Rugby   **Position:** Utility back
Height: 1.71m   **Weight:** 80kg
Caps: 2   **Points:** 5 – 1T

LEE DICKSON

Club: Northampton Saints **Position:** Scrum half
Height: 1.78m   **Weight:** 85kg
Caps: 9   **Points:** 0

MAKO VUNIPOLA

Club: Saracens   **Position:** Prop
Height: 1.8m   **Weight:** 130kg
Caps: 9   **Points:** 0

PLAYER PROFILES

MANUSAMOA TUILAGI

Club: Leicester Tigers **Position:** Centre
Height: 1.85m **Weight:** 112kg
Caps: 21 **Points:** 50 – 10T

MARLAND YARDE

Club: London Irish **Position:** Wing
Height: 1.83m **Weight:** 95kg
Caps: 1 **Points:** 0

MATT KVESIC

Club: Gloucester Rugby **Position:** Flanker
Height: 1.86m **Weight:** 104kg
Caps: 2 **Points:** 0

MIKE BROWN

Club: Harlequins **Position:** Full back
Height: 1.83m **Weight:** 89kg
Caps: 18 **Points:** 0

OWEN FARRELL

Club: Saracens
Height: 1.88m
Caps: 16

Position: Fly half/Centre
Weight: 96kg
Points: 154 – 11C, 43PG, 1DG

TOBY FLOOD

Club: Leicester Tigers
Height: 1.84m
Caps: 57

Position: Fly half
Weight: 92kg
Points: 299 – 4T, 39C, 66PG, 1DG

TOM CROFT

Club: Leicester Tigers
Height: 1.98m
Caps: 38

Position: Flanker
Weight: 105kg
Points: 20 – 4T

TOM WOOD

Club: Northampton Saints
Height: 1.95m
Caps: 20

Position: Flanker
Weight: 109kg
Points: 0

TOM YOUNGS

Club: Leicester Tigers
Height: 1.75m
Caps: 9

Position: Hooker
Weight: 102kg
Points: 0

(Stats correct as at July 2013)

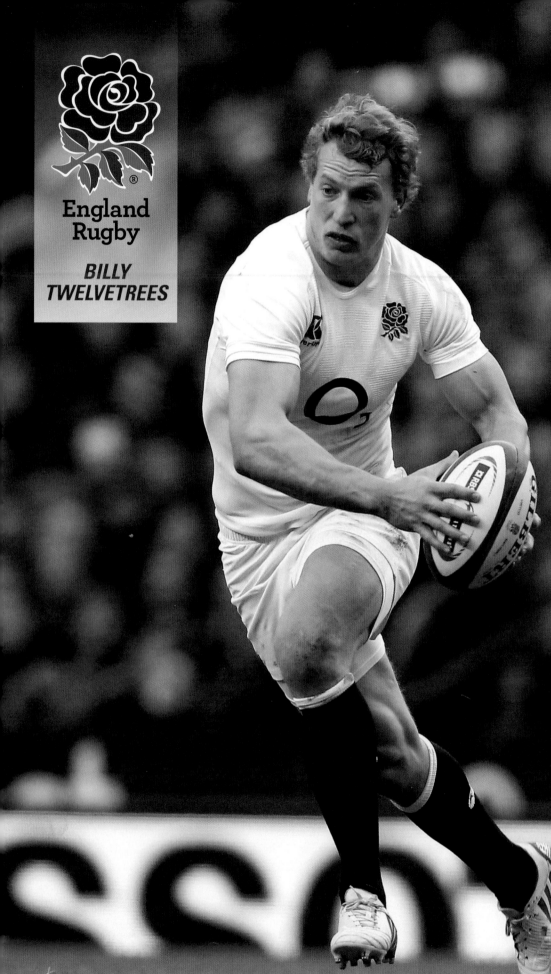

England Rugby

**BILLY
TWELVETREES**

Quiz Answers

Spot the Difference (page 15)

The Big England Rugby Quiz (page 17)

1. Auckland; 2. New Zealand and France; 3. New Zealand and Australia; 4. Argentina; 5. Twickenham; 6. A kind of kick from the hand – i.e. not a place kick; 7. By raising his flag; 8. Billy Twelvetrees; 9. South Africa; 10. Leicester Tigers; 11. Australia; 12. France; 13. 82,000; 14. Number 2; 15. New Zealand; 16. Owen Farrell; 17. Two; 18. Harlequins; 19. Scotland; 20. Number 13.

Spot the Ball (page 33)

The real ball is No.3!

Word Search (page 39)

T	L	K	G	X	K	Y	E	L	K	C	U	R	E
H	B	L	C	L	D	R	Z	T	K	C	D	G	W
Y	C	N	M	I	K	C	L	C	A	W	D	Z	J
O	D	J	L	L	K	F	S	L	A	U	X	R	N
U	B	R	O	W	N	R	C	H	J	T	E	T	R
N	H	R	W	T	Z	U	F	F	O	K	C	K	Y
G	C	E	N	B	T	Q	V	L	N	R	T	H	E
S	A	G	V	T	W	T	S	A	G	P	T	N	L
F	O	N	A	T	C	N	L	G	S	K	K	S	T
D	C	I	T	E	O	F	Y	M	T	N	B	J	R
R	W	W	N	C	Y	K	Q	G	N	W	N	L	A
Z	K	T	L	D	P	A	R	L	I	N	G	N	H
H	R	A	R	D	L	A	N	C	A	S	T	E	R
E	F	L	D	T	R	I	H	S	S	L	C	J	M

Guess Who? (page 43)

1. Danny Care; 2. Mike Brown; 3. Owen Farrell; 4. Geoff Parling.